G000167117

GET VISUAL!

Win clients and grow your business
with visual models

STREAMLINE STANDOUT SCALE

RENÉE HASSELDINE

For the business owner with complex solutions and an abundance of knowledge and ideas …

First published by Ultimate World Publishing 2021
Copyright © 2021 by Renée Hasseldine & Eventology Pty Ltd

ISBN

Paperback: 978-1-922597-23-6
Ebook: 978-1-922597-24-3

You may only use the techniques shared in this book in your own
business. If you wish to use Think RAPT® with your clients, please
contact us about our certification & licensing program.

ThinkRAPT.com

Cover design: Taylor & Grace
Layout and typesetting: Ultimate World Publishing
Editor: Marinda Wilkinson

Ultimate World Publishing
Diamond Creek,
Victoria Australia 3089
www.writeabook.com.au

TESTIMONIALS

This book demonstrates how to showcase your proven methodologies and the outcomes you create for your clients using visual models. Read it. And more importantly, take action on what you learn.

Glen Carlson
Co-Founder of Dent Global

This system seriously changed the way we do business! By using our visual models, everything we do now is on-brand, streamlined and consistent.

Amy Revell
Author, Speaker, Podcast Host and
Owner of The Art of Decluttering

Want to cut through the noise? Run, don't walk to grab a copy of Renée Hasseldine's *Get Visual!* Her methodology is cutting edge and a must-read if you want to tap into her wisdom.

Annette Densham
Journalist and Writer, The Audacious Agency

An ingenious model, which provides a simple solution to the seemingly complex task of building and scaling a business. I would recommend it to any entrepreneur or intrapreneur who wants to be successful.

Caitlin Johnston
Intrapreneur & Account Executive, J2 Group

Ever wished you could succinctly and simply share your zone of genius with prospects, so they 'get it' and transform (almost magically) into clients who stay loyal and refer others to you? If so, then Renée's *Get Visual!* book is the only business book you will ever need!

Cathryn Warburton
The Legal Lioness, International Award-Winning Lawyer, Business Mentor & Author

Taking complex ideas and making them simple and executable is difficult to do. That's what *Get Visual!* is all about. This book is for anyone wanting to leverage, make a big impact and move their ideas to IP.

Dr David Dugan
Founder, Abundance Global and Co-Author of
Bullet Proof Business

The way Renée extracted the million thoughts in my head and turned it into something magic on paper is simply genius. Buy this book. Read this book. Let this book change your business forever.

Dixie Crawford
Managing Director, Source Nation

Simple yet profound. Inspiring. Doable. This book is an absolute godsend in today's 'zoomiverse'. You MUST visualise your message. Go get it and apply it!

Doris Möhsl
International Trainer, Coach & Psychotherapist

No more lengthy proposals and pitches. Visual models are the new black! Highly recommended!

Jodie Willmer
Co-Founder and Business Mentor,
Happy Changemakers

Renée is one of the most amazing people on the planet. Her life's work makes any business owner's life easier as she gives them proven systems that are essentially a pathway for their clients to give them more money! I highly recommend you not only get this book, but her other works as well. She really gives away gold for the price of pennies.

Johann Nogueira
Founder of Business Authorities

If you want to IGNITE your business, read this book and follow this system.

John Lee Dumas
Host of Entrepreneurs on Fire & Author of
The Common Path to Uncommon Success

In an overwhelming world, you need to find a way to stand out and *Get Visual!* certainly helps you more easily explain what you do, your approach and process and enables your potential customers to visualise the outcome of working with you. This is an essential tool for entrepreneurs and business leaders who have a unique proposition they want to share with the world.

Lauren Clemett
Co-Founder of The Audacious Agency

If you want to win more clients and supercharge your business, then you need this system. Banish the waffle in those bespoke proposals and let your genius shine. 'Get Visual' now!

Linda Garnett
Director, Stellar Partnerships

If you are a coach, consultant or expert in your field and you haven't implemented the strategies that Renée shares then it is guaranteed you are leaving value on the table.

Lisa Brincat
Global Sisters Coaching Lead

The Think RAPT System is the fundamental business pitch they forgot to teach you in business school. Master this system, and you'll never have to worry about standing out in a crowded market again.

Martin Traz
Business Strategist & Expert Legacy Builder

This book will turn the complex thing that you do, into a simple visual system your clients will understand.

Natasa Denman
CEO, Ultimate 48 Hour Author

A terrific 'how to' for clarifying your own ideas and articulating them to those who need to know. Renée has thought deeply and articulated clearly her ideas, to help you do the same.

Peter Canny
Practice Leader, el camino

Renée is really clever. She'll help you to see what you can't and put it together in a way that the world can see it too. Bust out the highlighter and get stuck into this book!

Sam Patterson
ICF Master Certified Coach, Creator SURF at One

Want to boost your business' desirability and scalability fast? Renée's essential guide to visual models is the answer you've been searching for!

Sarah Birken
Strategic Sensemaker Consultant

How do you know when you've read a great book? Well, after you've read it, it stays on your desk and is never out of arms-length. It becomes a resource that you keep going back to for ideas and inspiration. *Get Visual!* is definitely one of those books.

Tyson E Franklin
Podiatry Business Coach

CONTENTS

INTRODUCTION

SO MUCH NOISE!

I don't need to tell you that we are constantly bombarded with information. The sheer quantity of information we are subjected to on a daily basis has increased ridiculously over time. In 1986, it was the equivalent of 40 newspapers per day. By 2007, that had grown to 174 newspapers worth of information.[1] Every. Single. Day. And I can personally attest to consuming a lot more information in 2021 than I did in 2007. You too?

---

[1] Assuming an 85-page newspaper. – Hilbert, M 2012, 'How much information is there in the "information society"?'. *Significance*, vol. 9(4).

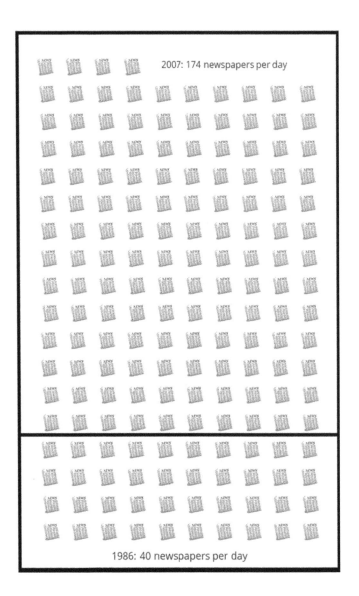

2007: 174 newspapers per day

1986: 40 newspapers per day

As business owners, this presents us with a challenge.
How do we actually cut through all the noise and get
our audience's attention?

THINKING, FAST AND SLOW

Research shows[2] that the brain uses two different systems to process information.

System 1 is FAST and automatic. When you see a STOP sign, System 1 recognises it instantly, before you even realise it.

System 2 is SLOW and requires conscious effort. Try to mentally calculate 27 x 36; no answer springs to mind automatically, but if you choose to engage System 2, you can probably work out the solution.

System 1 produces answers quickly and efficiently and values things that 'feel right'. It works almost instantly, and without effort. For example, visual models, things that rhyme, alliteration and acronyms will appeal to System 1. It makes snap judgements, but it doesn't always get things right.

System 2 is slow and cumbersome, but its solutions are usually better and it is the only brain system that can tackle complex, sophisticated problems. It takes deliberate effort, and overworking this system will make someone feel tired and disengaged.

---

[2] Kahneman, 2012, *Thinking, Fast and Slow,* Penguin Press.

Your audience will need to engage their System 2 to understand the importance and relevance of what you can offer them. However, before they do that, they will make a snap judgement of you and what you have to offer, using their System 1. This is your opportunity – grab your audience's attention and get them excited with visual models.

Once they are engaged and interested in what you have to say, they are more likely to put in the effort to turn on System 2 and carefully consider the all-important details of how you can help them.

THE BRAIN LOVES VISUALS

A visual will cut through all that noise faster than a whole bunch of words. Why? Because the brain loves visuals. It actually dedicates more than 50% of its resources to processing visual information.[3] The rest of the brain processes all the other stuff. By tapping into what the brain is optimised to work with, we can help our clients to understand what we do faster.

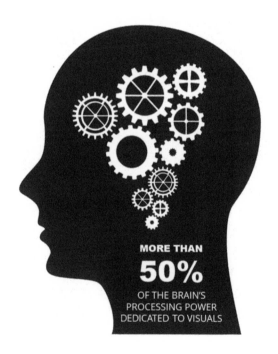

[3] Medina, 2014, *Brain Rules*, 2nd edn, Pear Press, Seattle.

PICTURE SUPERIORITY EFFECT

Our brains love to process visual information, and they also love to retain and recall it! In fact, if you give an audience just text or just audio, three days later, they're only going to remember about 10% of that information. But, if you give them text plus pictures, they remember 65% of it![4] This phenomenon is known as the Picture Superiority Effect. So if you want to remain top of mind for your audience, using visual models is a very powerful way to do that.

MEMORY RETENTION AFTER 3 DAYS

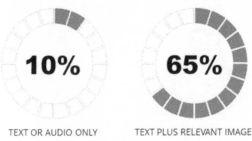

TEXT OR AUDIO ONLY   TEXT PLUS RELEVANT IMAGE

And that's what we'll be exploring together in this book.

So let's do it.

Grab a cuppa and let's Get Visual!

---

4 Paivio & Csapo, 1973, 'Picture superiority in free recall: Imagery or dual coding?' *Cognitive Psychology*, vol. 5 (2), pp. 176–206.

PART 1

REAP THE REWARDS

BENEFITS OF
Think RAPT®

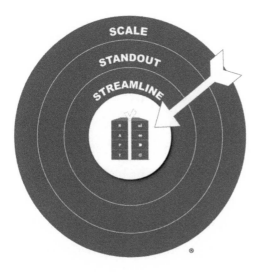

In this book, I will share with you our award-winning Think RAPT® system. With your own Think RAPT® system at the core of your service-based business, you can **streamline** your service delivery, **standout** in a competitive market and **scale** your operations.

STREAMLINE

'We're constantly reinventing the wheel with every client. As the founder, everything is inside my head and everything relies on me. It's exhausting, not very profitable and it's not sustainable.'

Our clients before they've created their Think RAPT® system!

Using the Think RAPT® system, your ability to deliver consistently high-quality services is streamlined, structured and standardised. This allows you to create content and products faster than ever before. By eliminating or reducing inefficiencies that cost you stress, time and money, you optimise the profit margin for each and every package that you sell, without sacrificing results for your highly prized clients.

Your Think RAPT® system forms the basis of every offer in your business. From social media content and webinars, to your highest premium offer and all the places in between. The core structure is there. No more staring at blank screens, creating bespoke proposals, wondering what to say on social media or how to structure your next keynote presentation. Service delivery and product development is totally streamlined.

Case Study: Rosie Shilo

Rosie Shilo is the founder and CEO of Virtually Yours and she really is a role model for efficient product development. Within eight months of creating her Think RAPT® system she:

- wrote two books
- created and sold out an online program
- launched a podcast
- continued to serve her existing clients.

All of this while working just two days per week! What an absolute superstar.

STANDOUT

'Our solution is quite complex. There is so much information that we need to communicate, so it takes time and a big conversation to explain it. We waffle and go round in circles trying to communicate our value proposition. People don't understand what we're saying and that means we don't have as many clients as we would like.'

Our clients before they've created their Think RAPT® system!

With a clear, visible and tangible value proposition using the Think RAPT® system, you boost your ability to stand out in your industry and attract high quality ideal clients. Being the creator of your own unique methodology provides an instant credibility boost and increases your ability to capture your audience's attention and win more clients.

No more waffling and stumbling over words when someone asks 'what do you do?' No more baffling your audience with jargon and losing them in the detail. Everyone on your team can be on the same page with consistent and powerful key messages that attract and convert clients.

Case Study: Anna Osherov

Anna Osherov is an #EVENTOLOGIST who teaches business people how to run successful events. Anna completed the Authority Accelerator program in June 2018 and it completely transformed her business. She went out the following week and donated a prize at an event. She had five minutes to get up and talk about what it was that she does and in that five minutes she converted 50% of the room into her half-day workshop. Are you kidding me? Five minutes. Fifty per cent conversion.

She used the pitch script I share in this book. Try it. It's gold.

Case Study: Katie-Jeyn Romeyn

Katie-Jeyn is an award-winning executive, bestselling author and creator of the Career Success Formula™ which is revolutionising how CEOs, executives, ambitious leaders and business owners accelerate their career or business in 12 months or less. When we met, Katie-Jeyn already had a successful career coaching practice with a $300,000 turnover providing bespoke customised solutions for her one on one clients and achieving great results. Katie-Jeyn wanted to scale her business and offer a 12-month group mastermind program. That's where we came in.

Katie-Jeyn now uses her Think RAPT® system to run her half-day workshop and upsell into her 12-month group mastermind program. The models themselves are used as the basis of both sales and marketing and service delivery.

Within 15 months of completing the Authority Accelerator program, Katie-Jeyn had built a million-dollar business.

Another absolute superstar. You blow my mind Katie-Jeyn.

SCALE

With your service delivery **streamlined** and the powerful ability to **standout** in your industry, you can **scale** and grow your business however you choose. Whether you want to serve more clients, create online programs, grow your team, diversify income streams, create recurring revenue, offer group programs or license your IP.

And … by developing these intellectual property assets and removing key person risk, you're in a better position when the time comes for an exit strategy.

So, if you have grand plans for your service-based business to have a massive impact on the world that is bigger than you, the award-winning Think RAPT® system can accelerate your journey.

ARE YOU GETTING THE RESULTS YOU WANT?

I started my consulting business in 2001 and I've met and worked with thousands of service-based business owners during that time. I've noticed two key things that are the difference between those who make it and those who don't:

1. Service Delivery
2. Audience Response

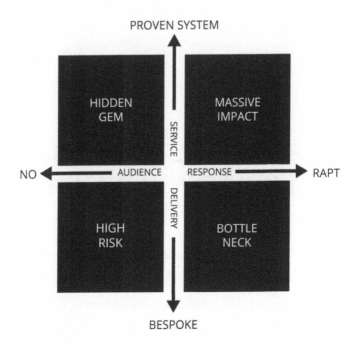

SERVICE DELIVERY

In the model above, service delivery is represented as a spectrum on the vertical axis. At one end of the spectrum, we've got bespoke solutions for each client, where we create an individual customised solution for their situation. Each time we work with a client, we unravel the complex web of knowledge in our brains, to deliver a solution and achieve the desired result.

We can absolutely provide quality results here, getting our clients from A to B, but we're not necessarily getting there in the most efficient way. It might look a bit more like this:

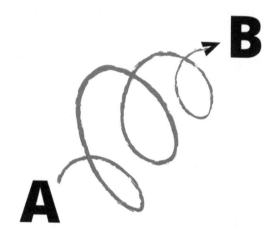

At the other end of the spectrum, we've got a proven system that is not reliant on any specific individual to be successful. A consistent, streamlined, reliable process, delivering outstanding client results every time in the most effective and efficient manner. No matter who on the team is delivering. We know that the shortest distance between two points is a straight line, and this proven system delivers that.

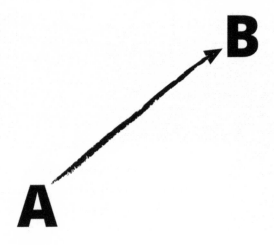

AUDIENCE RESPONSE

On the horizontal axis, we've got audience response. How does our audience respond to our sales and marketing? How do they respond to our proposals, presentations and pitches?

For example, you're at a networking event and you meet someone for the first time, who fits your ideal client profile. They ask you what you do and you give them your elevator pitch. How do they respond?

At one end of the spectrum, it's a 'hell no'. Their eyes glaze over, or they're looking over your shoulder to find someone else to go and talk to. They can't get away fast enough. They are definitely not interested, based on what you have shared. In a less dramatic example, they might simply be scrolling past you on social media.

At the other end of the spectrum, they're totally 'RAPT'. You share what you do and they say, 'That sounds amazing. That's exactly what I need. Tell me more. How can I work with you?'

For both axes, chances are, the reality is somewhere in between those two extremes.

HIGH RISK

If we're providing bespoke solutions and our audience is not buying, we're in trouble.

In the bottom left quadrant, every time we get a new client, we're designing a bespoke solution. We're having to create individual proposals every time we've got a new lead, which means conversion takes longer. Attracting and converting clients is hard work and slow. Delivering bespoke solutions is time intensive and focused. It can be difficult to juggle both activities at the same time, so we end up doing one at a time and dropping balls. It's a very lumpy, up and down, scary, high-risk way of doing business.

HIDDEN GEM

If we've got a proven system, but our audience is not buying, then we've got a hidden gem.

We've got the opportunity to convert that treasure into something more sustainable.

We could be sitting on a gold mine. There's potential there, ready to be unlocked. What we need to succeed, is an ability to stand out in our industry and attract and convert clients as a market leader. Clearly articulating our value proposition is the key.

BOTTLE NECK

If we're reinventing the wheel for every client, chances are, we'll be under the pump.

If we're great at bringing those new clients in, but then each client project is labour-intensive, we've got a bottleneck problem. There's massive key person risk. What happens if we get sick?

Even if we've got a team, they often still rely on us for key information and the clients insist on speaking to us.

Our ability to grow is limited by our personal capacity and there are only so many hours in the day.

Creating a proven system is the key.

MASSIVE IMPACT

Proven systems and a rapt audience mean profitably making a difference for more clients.

This is where we're having a massive impact. Getting paid to do work we love, the way we love to work, with people we love working with. We've got the systems, sales and marketing in place so that we can achieve it all, without the stress and uncertainty.

To achieve our mission long term, we need to have that proven system and the ability to attract and convert ideal clients time and time again.

Here's the great news ... No matter which quadrant you're currently sitting in, there's one thing that will accelerate your ability to have a massive impact faster than any other. That's creating your own Think RAPT® system.

Doing this ONE THING, will improve your audience response and service delivery faster than anything else.

After decades in business, I don't believe in magic bullets ... but this sure does come close!

PART 2

WHAT YOU NEED

HIGH QUALITY VISUAL MODELS

When creating quality visual models for your business, there's a bit more to it than just taking everything out of your head and sticking it into one visual model. That's what I like to call a recipe for a dog's breakfast!

This is a dog's breakfast. Avoid at all costs.

You can also end up with a dog's breakfast if you create your visual models in isolation. Even though I create quality visual models for others, I never create models for myself without quality feedback.

I need to have my models reviewed by an expert. I need them to see what I cannot see and point it out to me.

Imagine, as an expert, I'm inside a cardboard box. I'm in here with all my expertise inside my box. I can only see what's in the box with me. I can't see what's written on the outside of the box. To get the complete picture, I need someone who can see what's on the outside of the box. Who can see all six sides and tell me what I'm missing.

I also need someone who's going to look at my dog's breakfast and tell me that Thriving Business goes in the Results Model. Sales and Marketing go in the Answers Model. Create Business Plan goes in the Process Model. And Profit goes in the Target Model. I need a Certified Think RAPT® Specialist who's going to give me honest feedback when I create a dog's breakfast.

When it comes to visual models, the Think RAPT®
system is the antidote to the dog's breakfast. There
are four types of visual models that we need for a
complete set and we've got the acronym RAPT to
remember these four models in the order we extract
and present them.

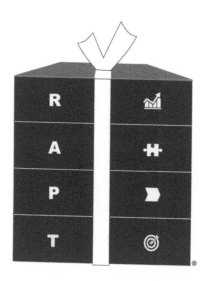

7 VISUAL MODEL PRINCIPLES

Before I introduce to you the four models, let's talk about the seven key principles for visual models in a Think RAPT® system.

- **Clarity:** the number one purpose of creating visual models and using them in your communications is to give your audience clarity. We want the messages that we are presenting to be absolutely clear and succinct.

- **Less is More:** do not overcrowd your models.

- **Consistent Words:** use a consistent number of words, usually between one and three, in each element of your model. If you've got three words in the first piece, then you put three words in every piece.

- **Language:** the language you use in the models must be clear, simple language that the intended audience easily understands and uses. No complicated, complex language or jargon. If you do, you're breaking the number one principle of clarity.

- **Alliteration & Acronyms:** alliterations and acronyms can be very sexy when they work, but there's a fine line between having a clever alliteration or acronym and a dog's breakfast. If you find yourself making up words to make your alliteration work, that's a red flag. It's nice when it works, but please do not force it.

- **Metaphors:** we can use our visual models to tell a story. You can do that by your choice of shape or how you speak to the model. Either way, the metaphor needs to be on-brand and appropriate for the target audience.

- **Appropriate Shapes:** make sure you choose an appropriate shape for the model type. I will share appropriate shapes for each type of model as I introduce the four models below.

Think RAPT® SYSTEM

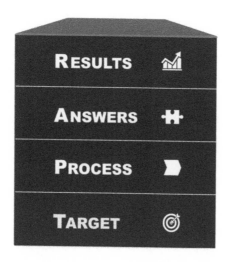

THINK HAPPY SYSTEM

RESULTS MODEL

The first model is the Results Model. The Results Model allows the audience to identify the current results they are getting, the results that they want, and the gap between the two. When they see that there's a gap between where they are and where they want to be, they're going to be motivated to do something about it.

We want to be use evocative emotive language in a Results Model. We want to be telling a story in a way that really captivates the audience's attention and inspires them into taking some action.

In addition to evocative and emotive language, we can also use icons to represent key performance indicators (KPIs) in your Results Model. Say for example, your audience really cares about how much income they're making, then you might use dollar signs to show how much income they make at each level in the Results

Model as you present it.

There are three different types of Results Model:

- The Hero's Journey
- The Spectrum
- The Matrix

One of these will be more appropriate for your business than the others. This will become clearer as we look at each of them in a bit more detail.

THE HERO'S JOURNEY RESULTS MODEL

The Hero's Journey-style of Results Model follows the classic storyline that we see in movies and books.

We use a simplified version of the Hero's Journey to create this style of Results Model.

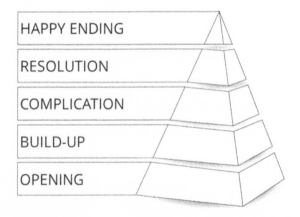

HAPPY ENDING

RESOLUTION

COMPLICATION

BUILD-UP

OPENING

There are five parts:

1. **OPENING:** Where does the story begin? What is the opening scene? Usually, the story begins before they're ready to work with you.

2. **BUILD-UP:** The story starts to build and there's some sort of progress that happens. Things are moving forward and developing.

3. **COMPLICATION:** This is when the 'you know what' hits the fan. Something goes wrong, there's a challenge or a drama. This is usually when there's enough pain for your audience to recognise, 'Hey, I've got a problem and I need a solution'.

4. **RESOLUTION:** The resolution is where you come in as the expert. You help them to solve the challenges they are facing.

5. **HAPPY ENDING:** The story ends with a beautiful happy ending. This is the result or outcome achieved.

Hero's Journey Shapes

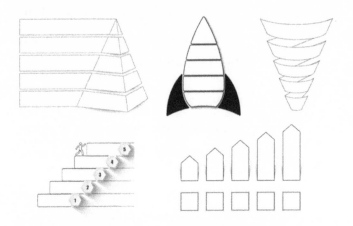

Appropriate shapes for a Hero's Journey are usually linear and show some sort of upwards momentum. There is a sense of progress and direction, showing that we're moving from where we are to where we want to be. We want to show that there's a shift happening and use a shape that will represent that.

When to Use

The following situations can indicate that a Hero's Journey-style of Results Model is right for you:

- Where your audience is an individual or small business owner.

- Where you are a role model for your audience, so that your story can be an inspiration for your ideal client's journey.

- Where one of your clients is a role model for your audience, so that a case study can be an inspiration for your ideal client's journey.

Results Model Example – Helen McIntosh

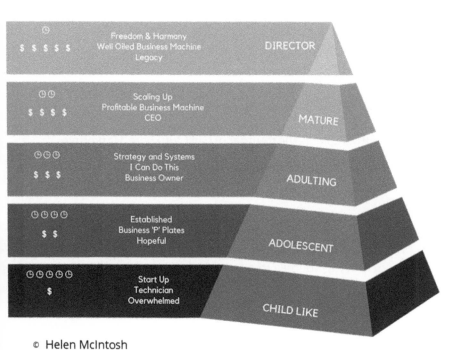

© Helen McIntosh

Helen McIntosh is the Operations Genie. She works with small business owners, specialising in strategy and systems. Notice the metaphor and choice of language, plus the use of icons to represent KPIs.

Results Model Example – Sally Stabler

© Sally Stabler

Sally Stabler is the founder of Get Out There Marketing. She is a marketing consultant who works in the tourism industry. Sally is personally very passionate about adventure. She loves to hike and so we've used the analogy of climbing a mountain when it comes to achieving success in a tourism business.

Results Model Example – Dixie Crawford

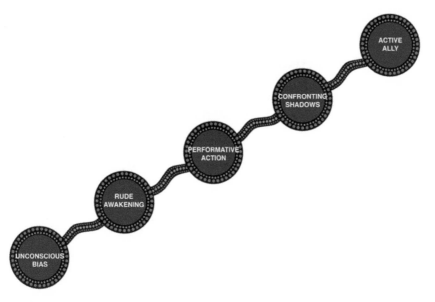

© Dixie Crawford

Dixie Crawford is an Indigenous thought leader and organisation coach. She works alongside Indigenous and non-Indigenous senior leaders and managers to create organisational cultural proficiency, identify and support the growth of Indigenous talent and achieve business outcomes. Dixie also runs a program for business leaders called Allies in Action.

Hero's Journey Dos and Don'ts

When using a Hero's Journey-style of Results Model, ALWAYS tell the story in the first or third person. NEVER in second person. If you're telling your own story, you tell it in first person. If you're telling a client's story, you tell it in third person. If you tell the story in second person, saying 'you do this and that' then all you have to do is get one tiny detail wrong, and you're going to lose the audience. And that's the opposite effect to what you're trying to achieve here.

Remember you're telling a story, a real-life story with real detail. Storytelling can be so powerful. Don't make it generic because you'll dilute the power of the story and model. You want your audience to be able to picture the person in the story and imagine it. It needs to be vivid enough that they can feel connected and identify with parts of the story that are similar to them. This model has the greatest potential to really build rapport and that 'know, like and trust factor'.

THE SPECTRUM RESULTS MODEL

The model above is an example of a Spectrum-style Results Model. There might be some style or branding variations, but essentially this is the shape. There are two ends of the spectrum, which are going to represent the extremes. At one end of the spectrum is the best-case scenario; the worst-case scenario is at the other end. And then you have the scenarios in between.

When to Use

The following situations can indicate that a Spectrum-style of Results Model is right for you:

- You and your audience are measuring the quality of something, e.g. relationships, visual models, corporate partnerships.

- Results may move up and down the spectrum over time, rather than following the same chronological storyline of a Hero's Journey.

- What is being measured can be at various levels at the same time.

Results Model Example – Visual Models

The Think RAPT® Results Spectrum above represents the quality of visual models that someone might have.

At the extreme ends, we have the best and worst-case scenarios. And then we have the 'in between'.

Let's say Bob has created a Results Model and it's awesome. But his Target Model is awful. He hasn't created his Answers Model or his Process Model yet. So they're absent.

The quality of Bob's visual models are not all at same level at the same time. And Bob doesn't need to start with awful models to work his way through a Hero's Journey experience to get awesome models.

He just needs to get himself a Certified Think RAPT®
Specialist and go straight to the best case scenario!

So, measuring the quality of something like visual
models works best in a Spectrum-style Results Model.

Results Model Example – Natalie Turvey

Natalie Turvey is a relationship coach and psychologist.
She specialises in helping people build unbreakable
relationships.

Again, at the extreme ends, we have the best and worst-
case scenarios. And then we have the 'in between'.

Let's say Jane has an unbreakable relationship with her
partner, but her relationship with her mother is broken.
She's currently healing her relationship with her sister.

The quality of relationships in Jane's life are not all the same level at the same time. And Jane doesn't need to start with broken relationships and work her way through a Hero's Journey experience to have unbreakable relationships. And we all know a Hero's Journey with a happy ending is not how relationships work in real life!

It's also highly likely that the quality of some of our relationships will move up and down the spectrum over time. They don't stay static.

So, measuring the quality of something like relationships works best in a Spectrum-style Results Model.

Results Model Example – Stellar Partnerships

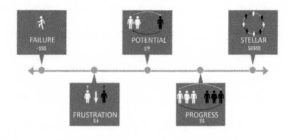

Stellar Partnerships is a strategic fundraising consultancy specialising in corporate partnerships. They work with organisations to help them establish and maintain high-quality, long-term corporate partnerships.

Their Results Model measures the quality of corporate partnerships. In this model, we are again measuring the quality of relationships, just in a different context. We're measuring the relationship between charities and their corporate partners. At the extreme ends we have the best-case scenario, being Stellar and the worst-case scenario being Failure.

THE MATRIX RESULTS MODEL

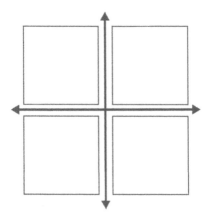

The model above is an example of a Matrix-style Results Model. There might be some style or branding variations, but essentially this is the shape. With a vertical axis, a horizontal axis and four quadrants.

When to Use

The following situations can indicate that a Matrix-style of Results Model is right for you:

- You are an established professional service business.

- You work with corporate clients.

- The outcome or results for your clients is determined by two main variables.

Results Model Example – Think RAPT®

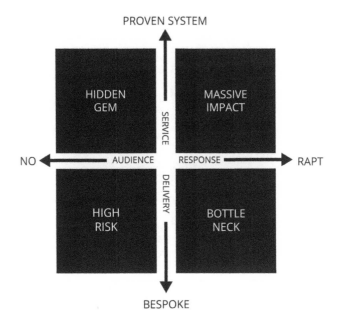

Here's the Think RAPT® Results Matrix. You've already seen this model earlier in the book, but I'm presenting it again here now to point out that it is an example of a Matrix-style Results Model.

The two main variables for this model are service delivery and audience response.

Results Model Example – Melanie Colling

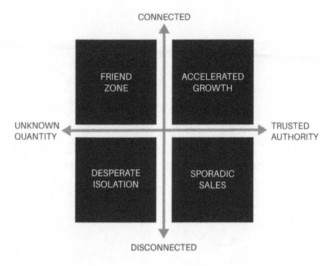

© Melanie Colling

Melanie Colling is the chief connection agent and partner at Experts On Air, the founder of Purpose Driven Projects and host of The Business Connections Podcast. She works with thought leaders who want to be seen as authorities in their industry.

The two main variables for her clients are how connected they are and their credibility as a trusted authority.

ANSWERS MODEL

The ANSWERS MODEL demonstrates the answers to your audience's challenges. It outlines what they NEED in order to achieve their desired results.

The sweet spot for an Answers Model is between three and seven elements. More than seven can feel unwieldy. Less than three will feel unsubstantial.

An Answers Model contains nouns, because these are the things that your audience needs to be successful.

The icons in an Answers Model are for aesthetic purposes. It's not like with the Results Model where the icons usually represent KPIs.

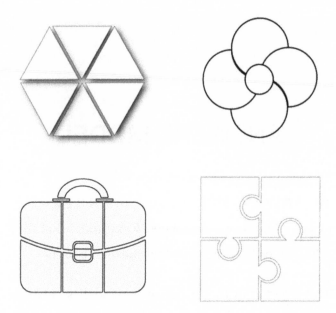

Appropriate Answers Model shapes are nonlinear, as shown in the examples above. We want something that looks like parts of a whole.

Some possible metaphors are:

- the things you need in your suitcase
- the pieces of the puzzle.

Answers Model Example – Melanie Colling

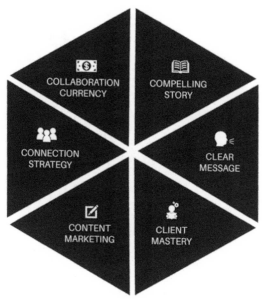

© Melanie Colling

This is Melanie Colling's Answers Model. You can see we've got some nice alliteration with all the C words. Notice that all these C words actually make sense and communicate clearly what Melanie is trying to get across. The icons are there for aesthetic purposes, but they're not providing any more information.

Answers Model Example – Dixie Crawford

© Dixie Crawford

This is Dixie Crawford's Answers Model. The shape and style intentionally represent Dixie's personal branding and her Aboriginal identity. Make sure your own models are on-brand in terms of the shapes, style, colours and fonts.

Answers Model Example – Sally Stabler

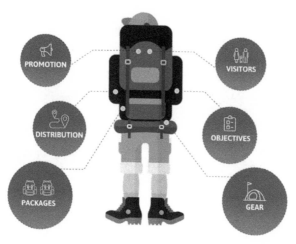

© Sally Stabler

Sally Stabler's Answers Model demonstrates all the things that you want to have in your backpack when you go hiking up that mountain (in her Results Model).

Answers Model Example – Stellar Partnerships

The Stellar Partnerships Answers Model demonstrates the key ingredients that need to be mastered by charities when it comes to establishing and maintaining successful corporate partnerships.

PROCESS MODEL

The PROCESS MODEL outlines your proven methodology, your unique way of getting your clients from A to B. It outlines your unique process for delivering results for your clients. It is the basis of your service delivery. The Process Model is all about ACTION. The things that need to be done. So make sure you use verbs. And just like in the Answers Model, the icons in a Process Model are there for aesthetic purposes.

The sweet spot for a Process Model is between three to seven steps.

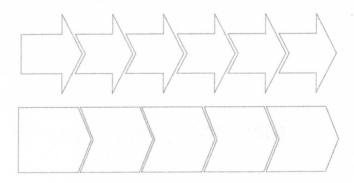

A Process Model should be linear. There may be some tiny exceptions to this rule, but there's a really important reason behind the linear shape for a Process Model.

Have you ever been in a taxi in a foreign city and wondered if your driver was taking you the 'long way' or 'round and round in circles'? You DO NOT want your clients to feel like that is happening with your solutions.

Remember, the Process Model is showing your audience how you're going to get them out of the pain that they're in.

If they're in enough pain that they're willing to pay you for a solution, then they want to get out of that pain as fast as possible.

The shortest distance between two points is a straight line.

A circular shape for a Process Model feels like you're going round and round in circles inside the pain. That's not going to be easy to sell!

Use a linear shape for your Process Model to reassure your audience that you will get them out of their pain ASAP!

Process Model Example – Think RAPT®

This is the Think RAPT® Process Model. Here you can see a linear shape, a numbered five step process, verbs and icons for aesthetics. We'll explore each of these steps in more detail in the next section.

Process Model Example – Melanie Colling

This is Melanie Colling's Process Model. It's a slightly different linear shape, with seven steps and some fabulous alliteration. You may notice that they're not all verbs. This was discussed during the extraction process and it was agreed that an exception would be made, as the ACTION for each step was still clear with the chosen words.

Process Model Example – Dixie Crawford

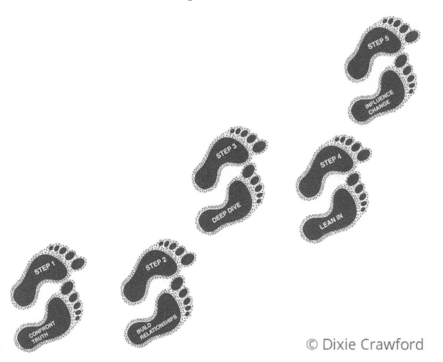

Dixie Crawford's Process Model is another example of shape and style reflecting personal branding. There's still a clear linear direction, a five step process represented by actual footsteps and verbs used to label each step.

Process Model Example – Sally Stabler

© Sally Stabler

Sally Stabler's Process Model uses stepping stones to represent her four-step methodology. We've got numbered steps and a clear beginning and end.

Process Model Example – Stellar Partnerships

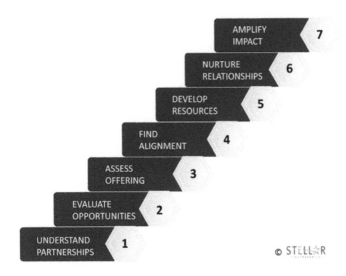

Stellar Partnerships' Process Model demonstrates their proven seven-step process for establishing those high-quality, long-term corporate partnerships. Using numbers, steps and verbs to demonstrate exactly what needs to happen to achieve the desired result.

TARGET MODEL

The TARGET MODEL highlights the benefits or KPIs that your solution is targeting. It shows your clients what they 'get' and answers the important 'What's in it for me?' question.

As per the Answers and Process Models, the icons in a Target Model are for aesthetics.

The ideal number of benefits in a Target Model is three. This is something that we have learned over time, with years of experience creating these models for clients.

What we've found is, if you have a Target Model with six benefits in it, by the time you get to it in your presentation, it starts to feel awkward. It feels like you're going on and on and on and throwing in a set of steak knives.

Three elements in a Target Model works best in terms of the rhythm of a presentation.

You get this, this and this. Boom. Drop the mic.

Short, sharp and punchy.

Appropriate Target Model shapes are nonlinear, as shown in the examples above. We want something that looks like parts of a whole.

If your audience is individuals, the benefits they are interested in are generally some variation or form of the following:

- Certainty
- Variety
- Significance
- Love/Connection
- Growth
- Contribution
- Clarity
- Relationships
- Purpose
- Results
- Passion
- Fun

If your audience is businesses, if you're B2B, the benefits they are interested in are generally some variation or form of the following:

- Time
- Money
- Stress
- Legacy
- Clients
- Leads
- Profile

Make sure you do your market research and use your audience's own words and language to label the benefits.

Target Model Example – Think RAPT®

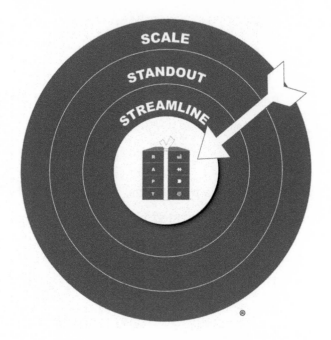

The Think RAPT® Target Model shows that when you put the Think RAPT® system at the core of your business, you're able to streamline the way you deliver your services, stand out in your industry and scale and grow your business. Boom, boom, boom. Done.

Target Model Example – Melanie Colling

© Melanie Colling

Melanie Colling's Target Model shows that when you follow her step-by-step process, you get influence, impact and income.

Target Model Example –Dixie Crawford

© Dixie Crawford

For Dixie Crawford's clients, who want to be active allies, the benefits of working with her begins with clarity. From clarity, you build confidence and then you're able to make the change in the world that you want to see.

Target Model Example – Sally Stabler

© Sally Stabler

When a tourism business works with Sally on their marketing, they get more visitors, more time and energy, and hit their revenue targets.

Target Model Example – Stellar Partnerships

When an organisation works with Stellar Partnerships, they get the right partners, profit, profile and the right people wanting to work in their organisation.

ANSWERING WHY, WHAT AND HOW

Each model in the Think RAPT® system fulfils a different role, but they are most POWERFUL when used together.

- The Results and Target Models are about **WHY** your clients should work with you.
- The Answers Model is about **WHAT** they need to succeed.
- The Process Model is about **HOW** you get results.

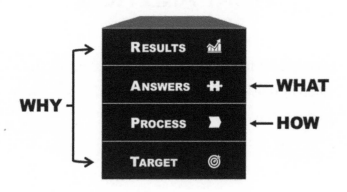

THE EMOTIONAL RATIONAL SANDWICH

When used together, the four models create an emotional-rational sandwich, that helps your ideal client say 'hell yes' to your solution.

The Results Model and the Target Model are the emotional bread. The Answers Model and the Process model are the rational filling.

By using all four models together, you answer both the emotional and rational needs of your audience in their decision-making process. People make decisions based on how they feel and they justify them with logic. By using all four models, you give your audience all the information they need to make an informed decision.

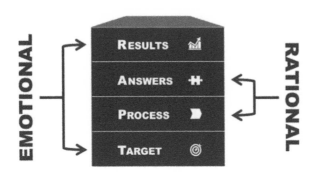

PART 3

MAKE IT HAPPEN

5 STAGES TO CREATING YOUR OWN Think RAPT® SYSTEM

STAGE 1: CLARIFY

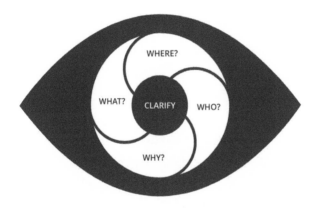

The first stage in creating your own Think RAPT®
system is to clarify the where, who, why and what.
Ideally, you would regularly address these questions
in your business. The purpose of asking them before
you create your models is to ensure your models are
based on the most up-to-date information and are
therefore more likely to be sustainable, relevant and
longer lasting.

WHERE?

- What is the reality right now? Where are things at in your business? What results are you currently getting? Think about this in terms of KPIs.

- Where are you heading? What is it that you want to create in your business? What is the vision for your business? And what are your targets in terms of KPIs?

WHO?

- Who is your audience?
- Who is your ideal client?

When describing your ideal client, don't write general demographics. Pick a specific favourite client that you totally loved working with and describe them. You may like to include:

- Name (this helps keep you focused)
- Education
- Job/Business
- Relationship status
- Kids

- Where they live
- What's going on for them
- Hobbies
- Social media habits
- Where they hang out

For example, Kathy works in a corporate job that she no longer enjoys. She's got a university degree and no kids. She's young and single and feels like she's not doing anything with her life. She feels like her work is pointless and it's starting to get her down and affect her social life. She wants to find a job that is meaningful. She wants to make a positive impact on the world. She does yoga once a week and checks Facebook multiple times a day.

The hobbies, social media habits and where they hang out are going to give you big clues in terms of WHERE you should focus your marketing activity. It is much easier to target your messaging where they already are, rather than trying to drag them somewhere else.

WHY?

Here we want to understand your ideal client's DEEP WHY. Why your audience needs you, wants you and will pay you money. This includes:

- Pain points: What are your ideal client's most painful symptoms that things aren't as good as they could be? What problems are showing up?

- Worst-case scenario: What is their worst-case scenario?

- Solution wants: What does your client want instead of the pain points?

- Best-case scenario: What is their best-case scenario?

WHAT?

- What is the result your audience wants?
- What do they want from you?
- What will they pay you for?

MARKET RESEARCH

I highly recommend you conduct market research to understand your ideal client's DEEP WHY and their WHAT. Conduct the market research via conversations, NOT in a survey.

Note their exact language and write that down, so you can reflect THEIR language in the models (record it and get it transcribed if you need to).

STAGE 2: EXTRACT

In Stage 2, you're going to extract your four models in the order of the Think RAPT® system. This is where we extract your four models from your brain.

Here's a reminder of the four models and the order.

EXTRACT YOUR RESULTS MODEL

To extract your Results Model, select the appropriate style from the three options mentioned earlier – The Hero's Journey, Spectrum or Matrix – and then follow the relevant instructions below.

Remember, we want the Results Model to be evocative. So dig deep into the emotions for this model.

OPTION 1: HERO'S JOURNEY

The Hero's Journey is used to tell YOUR story or the story of a client as a CASE STUDY.

To extract the relevant information for each stage of this story:

- Focus on ONE specific hero (you or your case study client).

- Think about what the hero of the story sees, hears, feels, thinks, knows and says.

- Describe it in as much detail as possible.

Draw a table like this to use for your extraction:

OPENING	BUILD-UP	COMPLICATION	RESOLUTION	HAPPY ENDING
Where does the hero's story begin? Take us back to the beginning.	What progress is made between the opening and the complication?	What is the typical scenario your clients are in when they come to you? (See Stage 1, Pain Points.)	Describe the transition between the complication and the happy ending.	What is the best-case scenario for your audience? (See Stage 1, Best-Case Scenario.)

Extract/fill in the information in this order:

1. Happy Ending
2. Complication
3. Resolution
4. Opening
5. Build-Up

Once you have extracted all this information:

1. Give each box a heading/title.
2. Which KPIs are appropriate to measure? Think about how these can be represented as icons in this model. (Note: These will likely be linked to your Target Model!) For example, time, money, clients, meaning, clarity.
3. Select a shape for this model and add in the labels for each stage.

OPTION 2: SPECTRUM

Draw a table like this to use for your extraction:

WORST CASE	REGRESSION	COMPLICATION	RESOLUTION	BEST CASE
What is the worst-case scenario for your audience? (See Stage 1, Worst-Case Scenario.)	What does going backwards look like?	What is the typical scenario your clients are in when they come to you? (See Stage 1, Pain Points.)	What does a resolution or progress towards the best-case scenario look like?	What is the best-case scenario for your audience? (See Stage 1, Best-Case Scenario.)

Extract/fill in the information in this order:

1. Fill in the Worst Case, Complication and Best Case from your Stage 1 information. You may need to expand on each of these by asking 'What does that look like? Feel like? Sound like? What are people saying here?'
2. Fill in the Regression.
3. Fill in the Resolution.

Once you have extracted all this information:

1. Give each box a heading/title.
2. Which KPIs are appropriate to measure? Think about how these can be represented as icons in this model. (Note: These will likely be linked to your Target Model!) For example, time, money, clients, meaning, clarity.
3. Select a shape for this model and add in the labels for each stage.

OPTION 3: MATRIX

Draw a matrix like this to use for your extraction:

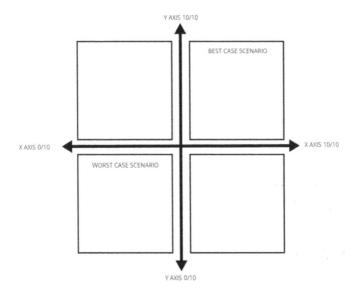

Start by filling in the best and worst-case scenarios from Stage 1.

Fill in the two main variables on your X and Y axes. These are the two key factors that will determine the results of your audience. Then label the extreme ends of each of these axes.

Fill in the scenarios for the top left and bottom right quadrants, based on the X and Y axis combinations.

If you have got this correct, either the top left or the bottom right quadrant should reflect your ideal client's Pain Points from Stage 1.

Once you have extracted all this information:

1. Give each box a heading/title.

2. Which KPIs are appropriate to measure? Think about how these can be represented as icons in this model. (Note: These will likely be linked to your Target Model!) For example, time, money, clients, meaning, clarity.

3. Select a shape for this model and add in the labels for each stage.

Results Model checklist:

- ✓ Refer to the 7 Visual Model Principles
- ✓ Is your Results Model emotive and evocative?
- ✓ Does this model apply to your clients? Work through specific examples.

EXTRACT YOUR ANSWERS MODEL

I highly recommend using sticky notes for the extraction of your Answers Model. One idea per sticky note.

To extract your Answers Model, begin with brainstorming the obstacles that get in the way of your clients achieving the results that they want. Once you've got the obstacles listed, go through that list and brainstorm the answers to those obstacles.

You might end up with a list of fifty answers that your clients need. So you'll need to group that list into categories. Aiming for between three and seven groups. Organise your sticky notes to create logical groups. These groups become the elements in your Answers Model.

Then, give each of those elements a label. Remember, you want nouns for the Answers Model. These are things that they actually need to master.

Select a shape for this model and add in the labels for each element.

That's it! Your Answers Model is extracted!

Answers Model checklist:

- ✓ Refer to the 7 Visual Model Principles
- ✓ If your clients master the ingredients in this model, will they be successful?
- ✓ An Answers Model is NOT about what they need to DO. That is for the PROCESS MODEL.
- ✓ Have you used nouns?
- ✓ Do you have between 3 and 7 elements?

EXTRACT YOUR PROCESS MODEL

The Process Model should show the step-by-step process AFTER your clients have bought from you. It forms the basis of your service delivery, whether done-for-you, done-with-you or do-it-yourself.

The Process Model shows how you get your clients from A to B.

- The starting point (A) comes from the Complication in your Results Model

- The end point (B) comes from the Happy Ending or Best-Case Scenario in your Results Model.

To extract your Process Model, brainstorm all the things that need to happen to get from A to B. One idea per sticky note. Remember this model is about ACTION. Things that need to be done. Whether your client does them or you do them, include everything that needs to happen.

You might end up with 106 things that need to happen to get the desired result for your clients. But nobody wants a 106-step process. So you'll need to group those actions into categories. Again, aiming for between three and seven groups. Organise your sticky notes to create logical groups. These groups become the elements in your Process Model.

Then, give each of those groups a label. Remember, you want verbs for the Process Model. These are things that actually need to be DONE.

Select a shape for this model and add in the labels for each step in the process.

That's it! Your Process Model is extracted!

Process Model checklist:

- ✓ Refer to the 7 Visual Model Principles
- ✓ If all the steps in this model are completed, will your client get the desired result?
- ✓ Do you have between 3 and 7 steps?
- ✓ Have you used verbs? (Doing/action words)

EXTRACT YOUR TARGET MODEL

The Target Model is best with FEWER benefits. Short, sharp and punchy. Three benefits is ideal.

To extract your Target Model, refer to the Solution Wants and Best-Case Scenario from the Deep Why in Stage 1. This should feed straight into the benefits you are targeting with your solution.

Organise the benefits into three groups.

Then, give each of those groups a label.

The Target Model should demonstrate what your clients GET.

Select a shape for this model and add in the labels for each stage.

That's it! Your Target Model is extracted!

Target Model checklist:

- ✓ Refer to the 7 Visual Model Principles
- ✓ Are these all BENEFITS that your client will pay for? (Not features.)

STAGE 3: PRESENT

Once you've extracted your four models, the next step is to present your models out loud using the presentation script.

The presentation script has two main purposes:

1. During Stage 3, you're using the presentation script to refine the models you extracted in Stage 2, before you send them off for graphic design. When you present your models to a Certified Think RAPT® Specialist, they will be able to make a range of tweaks and improvements and ensure you avoid going to market with a dog's breakfast. We tend to find that the quality of models extracted in isolation is about 60–80%. Once they've been reviewed by a Certified Think RAPT® Specialist, they'll be at 95%+. If you've worked

with a Certified Think RAPT® Specialist for the whole process, there will be less tweaking required at Stage 3, but it is still an important part of the refinement process.

2. In the future, the presentation script can be used in all your sales and marketing. From sales brochures and proposals, to keynote speeches and pitch presentations.

PRESENTATION SCRIPT

Even though the combination of the Think RAPT® system and presentation script has consistently high conversion rates, the overall tone of the presentation script is educational. You are always adding value, teaching and sharing, NOT 'selling'.

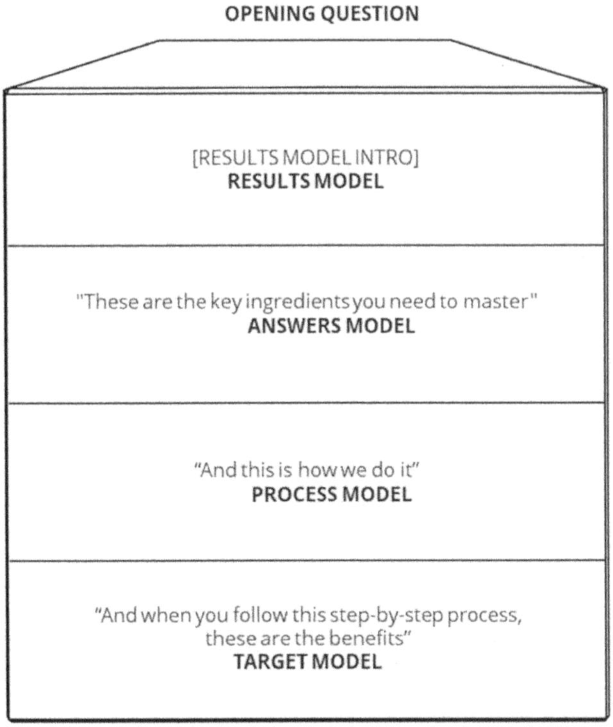

OPENING QUESTION

[RESULTS MODEL INTRO]
RESULTS MODEL

"These are the key ingredients you need to master"
ANSWERS MODEL

"And this is how we do it"
PROCESS MODEL

"And when you follow this step-by-step process,
these are the benefits"
TARGET MODEL

The presentation script is shown in the diagram above. Some further information on the Opening Question and Results Model Introduction are provided below.

OPENING QUESTION

Start your presentation with an opening question. The purpose of the opening question is to get your audience's attention, engage them and ask them something that you know your ideal client will say 'YES' to.

The type of question you ask will depend on the psychology of your target audience. Are they more likely to respond to the pain they're moving away from or the results they're moving towards?

For example, if you work with people who've experienced trauma, it can be very difficult for someone who is in serious pain to aspire to a grand happy ending. They just can't see that far ahead. You need to start with a safer question that they can comfortably say yes to.

If you're working with motivated business owners with grand plans to scale their operations, they're more likely to acknowledge their grand vision.

You know your audience best AND you may like to test out a few different questions to gauge audience response. Have some fun with it.

When you ask your opening question, raise your hand nice and high to show the audience how you want them to respond. When you get this right, everyone in the audience will raise their hand and you'll have their attention.

Here are some examples of both types of questions:

AWAY FROM PAIN	TOWARDS RESULTS
• Have you ever felt [PAIN POINT]? • Some days, do you just think [COMMON COMPLAINT]?	• Who would like more [TARGET BENEFITS]? • Who here would like [RESULT OR OUTCOME YOUR CLIENTS WANT]?

RESULTS MODEL INTRO

The way you introduce the Results Model depends on the type of model you have.

For example:

- **Hero's Journey:** 'I started ... ' OR '[NAME] started ...' Continue telling the story.
- **Spectrum:** 'The quality of our [WHAT IS MEASURED] can be shown on a spectrum. At one end of the spectrum, we've got ...'
- **Matrix:** 'To achieve [RESULT], you need [X AXIS] & [Y AXIS]. If you've got [X AXIS 0/10] AND [Y AXIS 0/10] you get ... '

Once your models are animated in a slide deck, you just click straight through your models with one sentence per element. You can easily get through the whole presentation in under five minutes. In fact, I think my client record is three minutes and twenty seconds!

And … the presentation script is like a concertina that can be expanded out to a 60-minute webinar or 90-minute keynote presentation – and even further, to a half-day workshop. The more time you have, the more detail you add. You can add case studies, stories, research, statistics and examples.

But the structure of your presentation, the bones of it, stays the same.

Once you've presented your models and tweaked them as required for the highest standard, you can send them off for graphic design and move on to Stage 4.

STAGE 4: PACKAGE

With your Think RAPT® system created, it's time to review your packages, to streamline the way you deliver your services and optimise your profit margins.

PRODUCT SWEET SPOT

When you're packaging your services, always aim for the product sweet spot.

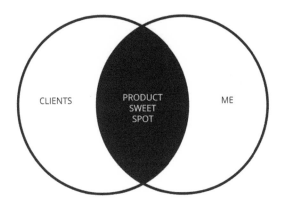

This means finding the balance between what our clients want and what we want.

CLIENTS	ME
On one side are our clients – their wants and needs and what they're willing to pay for. And there's no need to be a mind-reader. Do the market research. It ain't rocket science! Just ask them.	On the other side is us. Our strengths, passions, zones of genius. How we love to work and what motivates us.
Ever heard the advice 'Ask your clients what they want and then sell it to them'?	Ever heard the advice 'Just follow your passion and the money will follow'?
If you create products that your clients want, but that don't overlap with what you love and enjoy, you'll be left resenting the work that you do.	If you create a product that you love, but that doesn't overlap with what your clients want, you'll be left with a product that nobody buys.

The sweet spot is the zone of overlap in the middle. Every product we create should fit into that sweet spot.

PRICE VS SUPPORT

Your Process Model forms the basis of all your packages. Ideally, at every price point, you include all the steps in the process. What varies between the price points is how much support the clients get.

For example, the clients paying top dollar for your premium services get the highest level of support from you. Conversely, people opting-in to your free ebook don't get the opportunity to 'pick your brain'.

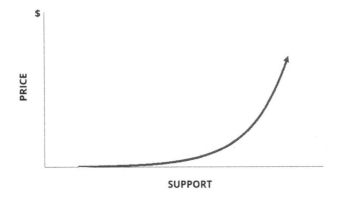

Price vs Support

PACKAGES AT MULTIPLE PRICE POINTS

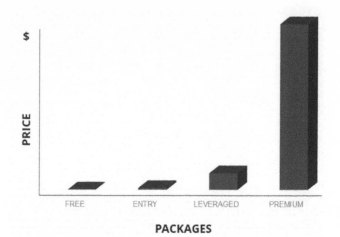

PACKAGES

Creating packages at multiple price points

It can be helpful to plan your offers using the four main categories shown in the diagram above and the table opposite.

Product Level	Examples	Price
Free Products	• Self-assessment based on your Answers Model • Video training based on your pitch script slides (around 10–20 minutes). Just jump into Zoom, share your screen and hit record. Boom! • Webinars – based on your pitch script slides. • Speaking gigs – based on your pitch script slides.	Free
Entry Product	• Book • Half-day workshop based on your pitch script, with a couple of exercises added in	Under $100
Leveraged Products	• Group Program – modules based on your Process Model.	$300–$5,000
Premium Products	• 1:1 service. Same curriculum as your group program, but provide support 1:1 or a done-for-you service.	$5,000+++

PRODUCT FUNNEL

Another way to look at your packages and prices is in a product funnel. The four models in your Think RAPT® system form the basis of every single level in your product funnel.

Let's look at how the relationship between the price and support works for the product funnel below.

For a $97 half-day workshop, participants get access to the expert during the workshop only.

For the $1,100 online course, they may get a single 1:1 session included, like we offer with our Game Changer package.

For the $11,000 VIP package, it may be a high-touch 1:1 coaching or consulting package. Or a done-for-you service like we offer with our Authority Accelerator package.

STAGE 4: PACKAGE

MARKETING CHANNELS

SPEAKING GIGS   SOCIAL MEDIA

FREE PRODUCTS

FREE TRAINING   SELF ASSESSMENT

ENTRY PRODUCTS

BOOKS $30

HALF DAY WORKSHOP $97

LEVERAGED PRODUCTS

ONLINE COURSE
$1,100

**PREMIUM
PRODUCTS**

VIP PACKAGE
$11,000

STAGE 5: CREATE

Stage 5 is about CREATING the assets and packages you've planned in Stage 4.

In addition to the graphic design of each model, you're going to need a slide deck with your models and a sales brochure. When clients work with us, we create those assets (and more) as part of our done-for-you service.

CREATE YOUR PREMIUM PRODUCT FIRST

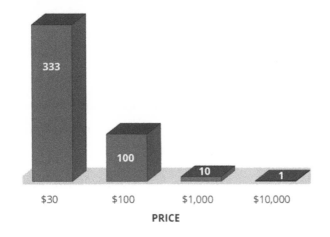

How many sales for $10,000?

When it comes to creating or upgrading your services to align with your Think RAPT® system, I recommend you prioritise the creation of your premium product. The diagram above shows how many products you need to sell at various price points to make $10,000. You only need to sell one $10,000 premium package, but you need to sell 333 $30 books to make the same amount. Decades of business experience has taught me that it is so much easier to sell one $10,000 package, than it is to sell 333 books.

So I highly encourage you create that premium product first, keep the wheels spinning in the business, generate decent profit and then you can look at building up the more leveraged income streams over time.

The great news is, that because all your products are based on the same Process Model, the videos, forms, templates, worksheets and other resources you create for the premium product, will be able to be repurposed for the lower priced products.

SOCIAL MEDIA MAPPING

One of the consistent challenges facing business owners I meet is coming up with high quality content for social media. As I've said, everything that you do now should be based on your Think RAPT® system – and that includes your social media content.

Here's some more good news … You'll never ever need to think 'What am I going to blog about this week?' or 'What am I going to put in my social media content this week?' or 'What am I going to write in my newsletter this week?' again! Because, with your Think RAPT® models created you can easily map out 18–24 months of content in under an hour.

Imagine you've got a six-step Process Model as an example. From that model, you can generate 25 weeks of content as shown in the diagram below.

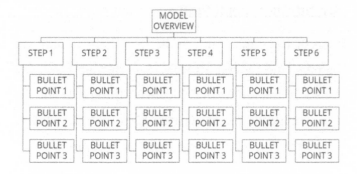

And when you multiply that by four models, you'll end up with between 50 and 100 weeks of content depending on how many chunks you've got in each model. At one content piece per week, you'll have 50–100 weeks of content in your four models. Then you can just start again because no-one remembers what you wrote a year or two ago.

So you can just map out all your content four all four models and then batch create your content at your desired rate.

My favourite way of doing that in a really leveraged way is to record 13 pieces of content once a quarter. 13 weeks in a quarter, 13 videos.

Each video is between 1–3 minutes long. So the whole batch of 13 videos can be recorded in under an hour. Once they're recorded, I hand them over to my team, they get them transcribed and repurpose the content in all the ways. Social media, newsletters, blog posts, articles. The best bit is, your job is done in less than an hour!

Isn't that awesome?

You can create this bank of quality, authority content based on your Think RAPT® system, give it to your team and move on.

CONCLUSION

So, there you have it. Our award-winning Think RAPT® system, which is designed to harness your genius for maximum impact. It really is a complete game changer to develop these four visual model assets for your business so that you can reach more people with your important work and mission and make an even bigger difference in the world.

When you put the Think RAPT® system at the core of your business, you will:

- Streamline
- Standout
- Scale

I can't wait to see how Think RAPT® accelerates your ability to shine even brighter. Perhaps I'll see you at an event, whether that's in person or online. Perhaps we'll work together to create your Think RAPT® system or you'll work with one of our exceptional Certified Think RAPT® Specialists. Perhaps you'll become one of our Certified Think RAPT® Specialists and be part of the movement to share this powerful system with the world.

Whatever the future holds for you, I wish you the very best.

And remember … YOU ROCK!

EPILOGUE

In 2020, we rebranded the business and upgraded our intellectual property (IP) to Think RAPT®.

The whole team was involved in the process as we worked with Darren Taylor from Taylor & Grace to ensure that our new brand was aligned with where we are heading. It was a massive effort, and I am so proud of what we achieved together. It really feels like a coming of age for the business and that the wheels are in motion for us to achieve our grand vision.

If you're familiar with my business, you may be wondering ... 'WHY?'

'Why did you rebrand?'

'Why did you change the name of the system?'

'Why are you writing another book? What is this one about?'

These are great questions.

Anyway, here's the story behind our rebrand, which should answer all your questions.

Not long after I developed the visual models IP in 2017, I started to see and believe in the potential for this system to be in training rooms all over the world, helping millions of people harness their genius. Replacing chaos and complexity with clarity and results.

But, the reality is, that I cannot possibly be in every single training room, helping businesses and teams to extract their intellectual property and turn it into visual models. It's just not physically possible and there aren't enough hours in the day.

So, I imagined that at some point, there would be hundreds, if not thousands, of experts trained by me or my team to use the Think RAPT® system. But I also knew that the Share Your Passion branding and the SEXY Models name of the system wasn't going to take us where we were heading. Because let's face it ... our licensees probably wouldn't be too keen to add 'SEXY Models expert' to their CVs and LinkedIn profiles.

So, knowing a rebrand was required, licensing the IP felt like a big, hairy, audacious goal with too many moving parts and too many unanswered questions. A rebrand is a huge undertaking and the ripple effects are huge. If you haven't rebranded before, think about every document, template, slide deck, worksheet, website, link, course, video, Canva design, social media profile and more in your business that would need to be updated. It's huge!

And so, as you might imagine, I wasn't in a hurry to make it happen. I figured it was a five-to-ten-year project.

And then COVID hit. And even though our business continued to thrive during 2020, there was a shift in perspective. We were fast forwarding our plans to train and certify specialists.

Suddenly it was all happening. We had two people who were wanting to beta test our licensing program and the rebrand was ON!

And we did it.

We rebranded the business AND created the certification training and licensing program for our Certified Think RAPT® Specialists.

It's a bit of a sleep deprived blur, but we actually did it.

The future is now! The 10-year dream is happening NOW!

We are now training and licensing Certified Think RAPT® Specialists to use the Think RAPT® system with their clients in two exciting ways:

1. Consultants working with businesses and organisations to help them with their external communications. Using the Think RAPT® system to help clients clarify their value proposition, messaging and service delivery system. This application of the Think RAPT® system is the focus of this book.

2. Consultants using the Think RAPT® system to engage internal teams in strategy, team building/development, and organisational culture and change. In this context, Think RAPT® is a powerful tool to co-create a path forward with clarity, buy-in and optimal

results. This application of the Think RAPT® system will be covered in a future book. Watch this space.

But we couldn't do that before the rebrand …

And the rebrand means the *Game Changer* book is out of date. So, this book brings you the new upgraded version of our award-winning Think RAPT® system.

When I first started my business in 2001, it was just me. It was all my ideas and my values and my vision.

Now, as I sit here writing this book in January 2021, there is a shared vision and shared values. Every single member of the team has contributed to the rebirth of this business together and we are stronger and more united than we have ever been. Think RAPT® is so much bigger than me and it's definitely not about me. It's about the work and the massive value it adds every day. Whether I can be there or not.

I encourage you to have big dreams for your business too. It is my intention that you will gain massive value from this book – and I can't wait to see where it takes you!

ACKNOWLEDGEMENTS

First, I want to acknowledge the traditional custodians of the land I live and work on. I reside and work on Wurundjeri land and I am writing this book on Gunaikurnai land. I pay respect and honour the ancestors of these lands and remain committed to listening, learning, growing and being together on what always was and always will be, Aboriginal land.

To my wonderful husband Ant. I'm so excited to thrive together with you this year and beyond. We've laid such strong foundations for our beautiful life together and who knows what this new chapter will bring. I'm so happy that you have this time to unwind, rediscover, explore and celebrate. Enjoy it my love. You deserve complete happiness and fulfilment.

Thank you for all that you are and all that you do. I love you inside out and back to front! Upside down and round and round!

To our wonderful daughters Callista and Cinta. Wow! What an inspiration you are. I'm so proud, lucky and blessed to watch you continue to grow as loving, resilient, creative, strong, thoughtful and kind humans. I love you to the stars and back.

To my superstar team. Thank you Stevie, Sol, Mel, Dea and Neha. I truly could not do this without you. I'm forever grateful for your commitment, your energy and ability to have fun getting shit done. Especially the stuff I don't want to do! We've already achieved so much together, yet I know that the best is still yet to come. It just keeps getting better and better and that's because of the contribution that each of you makes every day. I'm so deeply honoured and blessed to work with you.

To our clients who have inspired me by who they are and what they stand for – I'll always be grateful for the opportunities to co-create with you. I get such a thrill from watching you use your visual models to fly high. Keep rocking superstars!

ACKNOWLEDGEMENTS

To our Certified Think RAPT® Specialists. I'm excited about what our shared future together holds and I'm grateful for your ability to apply Think RAPT® in ways that I haven't even imagined yet. Together we can reach millions of people and help them harness their genius for maximum impact. Look out world. Here we come!

To Joy Fairhall at Izadrm, Golden Beach, Victoria, Australia. Thank you so much for providing a beautiful place for me to write this book, where I can swim in the ocean when I need a break. And, of course, for the orgasmic food, love and support to get this done.

To Natasa Denman, Marinda Wilkinson, Nikola Boskovski and the team at Ultimate World Publishing, thank you for your commitment to delivering and publishing this book to my very high standards. I'm so grateful for your patience during this process.

To Darren Taylor, Sarah Wilson and the fabulous team at Taylor & Grace. Thank you for working your magic and totally nailing the book title and cover design. Love your work.

ABOUT THE AUTHOR

Renée Hasseldine is the founder and CEO of Think RAPT. Think RAPT® enables small businesses, consultants, experts and thought leaders to wrap up complex thoughts and ideas into powerful visual models so that they can streamline, stand out and scale their businesses. Her knack for extracting and unpacking thoughts and turning them into clear, must-have solutions is sheer genius.

After graduating from the University of Melbourne, she began her career in the corporate world before establishing her own consulting business in 2001. Since then she has worked with clients from around the world, developing their intellectual property using her award-winning system.

As a speaker, Renée has inspired audiences around Australia and internationally, both online and in person, with her infectious enthusiasm and her commitment to adding massive value to every audience she meets. She has run six national tours in Australia, which involved hosting and facilitating half-day workshops and guest speaking at events in Melbourne, Sydney, Adelaide, Hobart, Brisbane and the Gold Coast. She regularly presents online workshops for audiences around the world.

This is Renée's third book, having achieved best-seller status for her first two books *Share Your Passion* and *Game Changer*.

FIND ME ONLINE

- Website: https://thinkrapt.com

- Facebook: https://www.facebook.com/ThinkRAPT

- LinkedIn Profile: http://www.linkedin.com/in/ Renéehasseldine

- LinkedIn Business: www.linkedin.com/company/ thinkrapt

- YouTube: http://bit.ly/ThinkRAPTYouTube

WORK WITH
Think RAPT®

To find out more about how you can harness the power of a Think RAPT® system in your business or become a Certified Think RAPT® Specialist go to thinkrapt.com

MORE TESTIMONIALS

Before we met Renée at Think RAPT®, we didn't really see the value of documenting and promoting our methodology and propriety processes. Working with Renée was transformative for our team and business – both in process and outcome. We now have a set of visual models which we are using to position us as truly different and as a litmus test to confirm fitness of new relationships. The models give potential clients assurance that we will achieve similar results for them that we have achieved for our past clients. But what's really exciting is that we now have systematised our core processes, which will allow us to scale very easily.

Darren Taylor
Managing Director and Head of Strategy and
Research, Taylor & Grace

Before working with Think RAPT, I didn't really know what I was doing. There was this lack of clarity and understanding on how I could separate different products, what the problems that I was solving were and the methods that I was using to solve them. I was just flying by the seat of my pants. Whereas now, I know if I actually go through my visual models, I can run a webinar on each of these things. It's clarity. Working with Think RAPT® is going to change a business, but more importantly, it's going to change you in the way that you think about your business and what you can offer people.

Dixie Crawford
Founder, Source Nation

I could not have chosen a better time than now to have worked with Renée through the Authority Accelerator program. As the world changes and I felt the call for my business to change, I hired Renée to help me with my signature system and models and I have been blown away by her level of genius in extracting what I know and placing it into a beautiful container from which I can serve my clients more epically, providing much more value and asking much higher prices. Going through this process has done so much more than just given me a signature system and the models to support it from sales through to delivery. I've been able to get even clearer on the book I'm currently writing and bring in elements that had been missing from it, that I was completely unaware of until doing this work. Renée and her whole team are super supportive and talented and I'm grateful for their contribution.

Anne Aleckson
SuperSelf Mentor

I love the way Renée took my ideas and simplified them, without losing the essence of what it is all about. She took all the words that I was using from my everyday work language and made it simple and easy for people to understand. The results are amazing and the pride that you get from going through the process and then actually having the output of that process is amazing. For me it was actually quite emotional because I felt someone finally understood what it is I'm trying to say. Renée came into it cold, but through the three sessions she learnt about what I do and used that understanding to make very simple models. So, for me, this is HUGE. It is a big thing – finally, somebody was able to put it together for me. I would say to people – just do it.

Elaine Hendrick
Director, Principal Consultant and Trainer, Elaine Hendrick Consulting

Renée Hasseldine is a genius at creating simple models for presentations. But that's not where it stops. I completed her Authority Accelerator program and got so much more from it than my simple models. I got a process to use those models in all aspects of my business from sales to marketing to presenting and delivering to clients and so much more. Renée is simply amazing!

Mary Wong
Speaker, Author, Mentor, Trainer, Optimal Life Solutions

Thank you Renée Hasseldine for your Authority Accelerator program where I was able to create intellectual property for my business systems. Creating my four models made a massive impact on my business. Within this course I identified my zone of genius as an event marketing consultant for business owners. Using my new models, I presented a five-minute talk to a room full of business owners to introduce my new workshop, 'Build Your Business With Events'. This very first five-minute presentation, using my new models had a 50% conversion of the room into attending my workshop. This has never happened before and I 100% attribute this success to the Authority Accelerator program that Renée has put together. This program has completely transformed my business. If you want to identify your zone of genius, extract your brilliance and leverage your legacy, I recommend you work with Renée!

Anna Osherov

Communicator, Co-creator, Vicarious Achiever

I invested in Renée's Game Changer course a couple of months ago. I am a systems and processes girl – I get their value. But typically, my systems and processes stay inside my head, and I struggle to articulate them to another person. Renée's course gave me a way to get my systems and processes out of my head! Most importantly though, the course enabled me to gain immense clarity on my flow and how the parts and pieces of my business fit together. And this is the most valuable takeaway for me. I now have a framework that scaffolds my creative process, and enables me to create products and services that are aligned with me and my brand. If you are seeking a better understanding of what you do in your business, check out Renée's course for sure!

Vidya Ananthanarayanan
The Life Adventure Guide Founder,
Totally Vidya Life Coaching

I worked with Renée to create my visual models a little while ago and presented them to a group of people for the first time today. Not only was I complimented on them by someone who creates professional presentations for a living, I also had another member of the group book in for an initial session on the basis of one model alone! The process of creating these models definitely challenged me, but with Renée's help I feel so much more confident in sharing what I do and how I do it!

Terri Adams-Munn
Coach and Chief Dreamer, Ten Thousand Dreams

Thanks so much Renée Hasseldine for your awesome brain and models! Loved the process and the clarity I now have ... hallelujah! It's an awesome course – get on board everybody. It's game changing!

Melanie Colling
Chief Connection Agent and
Partner at Experts On Air,
Founder of Purpose Driven Projects and co-host
of The Business Connections Podcast

I recently joined Renée Hasseldine's Game Changer course and since I created the models it is SOOOOO much easier to communicate what I do. I can tell my story easily. I have a quick elevator pitch and have created workshops, webinars and posts from just the words of each model. I'm just about to do a workshop this weekend using the five keys you need to master so you can move through resistance to ease and prosperity. Exciting.

Louise Geary
Founder, Activate You

Last week my husband Brian won your book and free tickets to your half-day workshop. I picked up the book immediately when I got home and started reading it and literally I couldn't put it down. I just wanted to let you know that I LOVED IT! It was like you were talking to me and I love your passion and your strategies.

Helen Micallef
Managing Director, Infinite Possibilities

Today I have been creating the four visual models from Renée Hasseldine's book, Game Changer. So excited to have greater clarity. They are drafted and ready for some internal review. Thanks, Renée for the great book.

Elise Stevens
Organisational Change Manager,
Author, Podcaster

Printed in Australia
AUHW021712251021
354195AU00010B/10

9 781922 597236